THE CALL OF THE
JESUS CHRIST

THE CALL OF THE
JESUS CHRIST

Farheen Saleem Akhtar

atmosphere press

Bismilllah Hirahmaaan Nira heeem!

To the love and kindness of Allah Subhana Tallah,
who chose me for this book to honor and express my
gratitude through the God-gifted Words, the lifeblood
of this humble author. Alhamdulillah!

I dedicate this book to the children of the Jesus Christ
and the beautiful memory of Her Majesty the Queen
Elizabeth II, whose legacy of unwavering devotion to her
people and her country has earned her our humble Love
and an unforgettable admiration in our hearts.

To the beloved and esteemed
Her Majesty Queen Elizabeth II.
With humble gratitude and deep admiration,
I dedicate this book of poems to you.

Your unwavering commitment to duty and service,
your grace and elegance, and your unwavering
dedication to the people of the United Kingdom has
been constant inspiration to the generation
of writers and poets.

It is an honour to offer these humble words
of tribute to a monarch who has given so much
to her country.

May your noble example continue to guide and inspire
us for ages and your spirit live on in the hearts of those
you touched with your kindness.
Rest in peace, Your Majesty.

THIS AFTERNOON

Be Of The Stars
Be Of The Moon
Be Of Thy Jesus This Afternoon

For seeds to water
The flower will bloom
Be Of Thy Jesus This Afternoon

Heaven be praised
The Bird's bride and Groom
Be of Thy Jesus This afternoon

For the love of December
For the love of June
Be Of Thy Jesus This afternoon

THE KNOCK ON THE DOOR

How can I imagine
A Knock on the Door
The Jesus of My

Like the Heaven comes to Floor
Take Me to the Children
Take Me to the Swore

Jesus Wept (*John 11:35*)
Who is there Thee of My a more

O The Children of Jesus Christ
Rejoice Evermore (*Thessalonian 5:16*)

How can I imagine
A Knock on the Door

CALL OF THE CHILDREN

I Don't Know where I am
I Don't know what I do
Here I call upon my Jesus
My Jesus where are you?

Days are passing by
Passing by the wind
Holding myself to your Arms
There is a song to sing
Singing to the sea
My Songs turns Blue
Here I call upon my Jesus
My Jesus Where are You?

The Children love You
The Children Need You
Please Come Back to Us
Children We seek You
Wandering around the skies
The Truer than the True
Here I call upon my Jesus
My Jesus Where are you?

Forgive Me

Forgive me if I am Sad
The Love of My Jesus So Bad
The Children are only My Hope
The Tear in Eyes So Mad

Forgive me If I am Sad

Forgive me If I am Sad
The Love of Children So Bad
The Bible is Only My Hope
The Tear in Eyes So Mad
Forgive me If I am Sad

Forgive me If I am Sad
The Love of the Bible So Bad
The Jesus Is Only My Hope
The Tears in Eyes So Mad

Forgive me If I am Sad

THE ROPE

Sometimes I wonder
If There was a Thunder
The Thunder of Fear
The Thunder of Hope
Would You Listen My Children
Would You Hold Up to the Rope
Would You Listen My Children
Would You Hold Up to the Rope

When No One Heard You
I Was There
For the One to Remember
Knows I am Where
Where The Wind Blows There is a Slope
Would You Listen My Children
Would You Hold Up to the Rope
Would You listen My Children
Would You Hold Up to the Rope
For The Sky is Blue
But Who Has the Light
Who Has the Courage
Who Has the Right
Never to Disobey
Never to Fight
I Left You My Children
To Thee Greater Than Might
For Hope Is in You, in You is the Hope

Would You Listen My Children
Would You Hold Up to the Rope
Would You Listen My Children
Would You Hold Up to the Rope

TELL ME HOW

I Call Upon My Lord

So Loud and Humble
With My Hands so together
And Heart so Crumble
O the Lord of the Great Moses
And Moses Question Thee Thy

Tell me How, How, How
When I can't say Why
Tell me How, How ,How
When I can't say Why

Destiny is there with the wind
Not every wind sings a song
Silence is there of the Jesus
What Have We Done So Wrong
O the Lord of the Great Jesus
And the Jesus Question thee Thy

Tell me How, How, How
When I can't say Why
Tell me How, How, How
When I can't say Why

The verse speaks the Bible
And The Bible answers me my
I waited Patiently for the Lord
He turns to me and hears my Cry (*Psalm 40:1*)

Tell me How, How, How
When I can't say Why
Tell me How, How, How
When I can't say Why

Stand I here to knock the door
If You can Hear the voice from the Sky
I will come if your door opens
Share a meal of togetherness a My (***Revelation 3:20***)
Tell me How, How, How
When I can't say why
Tell me How, How, How
When I can't say why

WHERE IS MY JESUS CHRIST

Sometimes I am Lost
Sometimes I am Found
To Whom I Begin
TO whom I Sound

For Here I Look for My Jesus
My Jesus Not Found

For Where I should GO?
For The Wind TO Blow

Thunder to Be Calm?
The Song to Sow?
For The Light into My Bible?
The Clock Turns to Sound?

Where Shall more I look for My Jesus
My Jesus Not Found

The word of the Thou
The Heart of the Thy
Gardens to the Valley
The Church of the Little My

A Bond to The Quran
Speaks The Bible of Thy
Silently knocking the Door
My Eyes in Tears a Down

Here I Look For My Jesus
Yes! My Jesus Is Found
Here I look For My Jesus
Yes! My Jesus Is Found

WISH MY JESUS A HERE

If the TIME turns back to me
Ask what would I care?
In My Silence within, I would Cry

Wish my JESUS A HERE!

For the world is so Empty
For the love every the 'Do' a dear
Takes me, he who, the love of my Beloved!
Wish my JESUS A HERE!

O The Lord of Heaven
Hear I your mercy a there!
In My Silence within, I would Cry

Wish my JESUS A HERE!

- Amen

WHEN I CAN'T SAY WHY (VERSION 2)

I call upon my Lord
So loud and humble
With My Hands so together
And Heart so Humble

O The Lord Of Great Moses
And the Moses Question the Thy

Tell me How, How, How
When I can't say Why

Destiny is there of the wind
Not every wind sings a song

Silence is there of the Jesus
Louds the Sacred Books an along
I waited patiently for the Lord
He turned to me and heard My Cry. (**Psalm 40:1**)

Tell me how, how, how
When I can't say Why

Stand I here to knock the door
If u can hear the voice of Sky
I will come if your door opens
Share a meal togetherness a My (**Revelation 3:20**)

Tell me how how how
When I can't say why

THE ASTRONAUT

Who am I wondering around the Mars
Who is in me keeping to the stars

For silence of universe retells a story
Behold the courage Behold the Glory

But what is there that shalt must look
What is Told and What is there the book

But sometimes something somewhat unknown!
What must we do before the trumpet blown?

Dime is in the vision
And clock turns Nine

Solution is there before you
When Wisdom is in the time

May how wish I peak inside?
Jesus Thee is in the Rhyme!

NO FAREWELL

For How Shall I See
The Bible of Thee
The Kept of Promise
The Belief in Thy Thee
For You are The Children
Seeking the Door
For How Much Longer
For How Much More
No Tree Is Green

No Violets Blue
The Word of Thy
Reminds me of You
No Farewell My Children
No Farewell Be True
Where You Believe Your Jesus
Your Jesus will be with You

The Talk of the Wind

O Who am I to see the Bird Sing
O Who am I to hear the Bird Song
Here I am in the love of my Jesus
And My Jesus Is Never Wrong
I wished upon the stars
I call upon the wind
The words were in the Heart
For the Tears in eyes to blink
For who are you My Lady

Knocking the door of the wind
Don't u know Your Jesus
For Jesus knows Your Glint
What Shall I answer
What Shall should the wind
For the love Of Jesus Is My
And He who has the Hint
I would keep knocking the door
For Years and Years and Many More
For the one day He would answer
I will dance my Bible a dancer
For one day he would answer
I will dance my Bible a dancer

THE BROKEN HEART

O Thee Thou of The Thy Jesus
I Make a Wish You Are My Jesus

The Lips Are Silent Eyes Cry Jesus
I Make a Wish You Are My Jesus

For I Know Not How to Mend the Pain
The Children Yours Loves You the Same

Blame I Myself the Words in Vain
The Children Your Loves You the Same

Forgive Me for It Was I The Hope
Still Believe I Them Hold on to the Rope

O Thee Thou OF the Thy Jesus
I Make a Wish You Are My Jesus

MY JESUS TAUGHT ME

The words those speak

The words those tell

How could I stumble

The lessons of the bell

My Jesus Taught me so well

My Jesus Taught me so well

The way to the father

The way to the mercy

The Door to the heaven

The Door to the courtesy

My Jesus Taught me so well

My Jesus Taught me so well

For so unforgiven I am now

And so forgiven I am to be

Mercy is in there of the father

Mercy is there within me

My Jesus taught me so well

My Jesus taught me so well

My prayers,ask forgiveness,My Father

The Creator,the Restorer,the Mercier

The memory I have of Your kindness

The Greatest, the Merciful, the Glorier

My Jesus taught me so well

My Jesus taught me so well

Here I am before the children

Here I am before the Holy Book

The words of faith I have taken

The burden of promise I took

My Jesus taught me so well

My Jesus taught me so well

I am well taught O My Father

For the best of myself to be

Greater you are than i

Greatest of all to be

My Jesus taught me so well

My Jesus taught me so well

(Amen)

The Tear in the Name Jesus

The Tear in The Name Jesus
Call upon The Sky

How shall I ask forgiveness?
To The Lord Of My

I Surrender to the pain
Whose woes not heard

The world would change a million

With Lord's one word

The Spoke of the Lord
The Glory comes to cheer

O The Lord Is The eternal!
Prayed so Loud The Humble Tear

The Spark Arosed
The Thunder Float

Behold the Glory

Behold The Told

The Giving of the Man
Is For a Reason

The Thirst for a wish
Steeps for a season

The Greed of the dark fears the light
Who is The Greater; Greater than i

O Where there the Sun
O There where the Bright

May You be Blessed

With A One Holy Word Provoken

May your Jesus with you
An every heart a broken

-Amen

The Little Valerie Laws

O Little Valerie
O Little Valerie
Hair so Golden
Eyes Like Mary
O Little Valerie
O Little Valerie
You smile like Jesus
The silence of Mary
O Little Valerie
O Little Valerie

For I am Thy Beggar
Never seen a Fairy
O Little Valerie
O Little Valerie
May You always be Blessed
The Wish to the God Fairy
O Little Valerie
O Little Valerie

THE LOVE OF JESUS MY WINE

The pain of the word
The songs you have heard
Shakes me to the time
Yes, the love of Jesus My Wine
You might be sad a little
I wish you see my heart brittle
When words become known to the unknown
Knocking the door before the dawn

I believe the day the star Will Shine
Yes, the love of Jesus My Wine
So let me be who May I am
Surrender to the wind who say I am
Finds Me why the shadow of Mine
Yes! The love of Jesus My Wine

THE PROMISE

Sometimes we are there a short of words
Heart speaks loud and Lips Never Heard
A Promise to make and a Promise to be
May How shall smile be a smile
Without the Thou of Thy Thee
For You are the children of Thou
And we are humble of His Thee
May the forgiveness be towards My
May the guidance Be Yours to Thy Thee

– Amen

TRY TRY AGAIN (VERSION 1)

When hope becomes the ladder
And the Belief becomes the song
Sing my Children up to the ladder
Come with me an along

Fire Must Shine Inside You
The Thirst of Spark to the Flame
The Word Shall Reunite You
Ask, Seek and Knock the door the Same

Try Try Again
Try Try Again

Let The lust of Gold be of the silver
And the silver shall remind You
The children You are of the cold
Never apart he who binds You

When deep of the Kindness
Sings the Mercy High above the song
The Angels dance the words
For the Kindness to Come An Along

Try Try Again
Try Try Again

For You have the trumpet
For You Have the Blow
The Mercy is in the rain
The Mercy is in the sow

When the birds look at the sky
And The Sky look back the birds
The Holding of the prayers in the Beak
The Hunt of the Dig of the Words

Try Try Again
Try Try Again

Speak you must of the Heaven
For AN earth far away a below
The sacred is not what you count
Wisdom surrounds the clouds to flow

For where stand your owe
Where stand the promise
The one you gave to the Thy
The One you gave to Thy Jesus

Try Try AGAIN
TRY TRY AGAIN

TRY TRY AGAIN (VERSION 2)

When You become Weak
The Hope Tweak
Try Try Again
When You become Hollow
The Dreams to follow
Try Try Again
When U can't sing
The love to bring (Romans 12:10)
Try Try Again
When U become a song
The Thou of Thy an Along
Try Try Again (*Matthew 18:20*)

When the word calls
The Hold on to the Falls
Try Try Again…

When You the Try
Then It Is You, the Try
Reason Thee of Yours
IS Reason Thee to My
Fly My Children
Must You Fly
Try Try Again

For Try You Must
To Heal the Thirst
The Jesus of Thy
To Hold Till U Dust

Try Try Again
For Try must you weep
The pain to sweep
Humble of Truth
Teared so deep
Try Try Again

When u know the truth
The Truth sets u free. (***John 8:32***)

Try Try Again

When two or three gather in my name
There am I with them (***Matthew 18:20 NIV***)

TrY TrY Again
Try Again and Again
And Then Try Again
For The Vow to The Jesus
Speak till Remain
Try Try AGAIN…
TRY TRY AGAIN

TRY TRY AGAIN (VERSION 3)

When The Clock mends the lines in hand
The Time, The Deed and The Sand

What Could Have Done What of The Can't
For The Rain to Fall and Sky to Thank

The Balance of Harmony and the Bells to Ring

Try Try Again
Try Try Again

Trust Must the Faith That Hold on to the Lord
The Angel, The Fire, The Abrahim

Fear Must There Only of the Lord
The Promise Made to Esteem

To Twinkle the Lamp Enlight the Meem

Try Try Again
Try Try Again

Hold on to the Bead for the Vision to Seed

The Noah, The Ship, The Dream

Walk the Forgiveness for Mercy to Witness
The Love of God the Beam

Sing The Sparrow the Songs Of the Tomorrow

Try Try Again
Try Try Again

Afraid Not of the Mistakes
The Adam, The Seed and The Trade

What Could have done and What of the Fate
For Mercy to Rise and Stone to Sand

For Every a Beginning There is an end

Try Try Again
Try Try Again

HOLD ME

O Thee Love of My Jesus Christ
Hold Me…!

The Words an Unspoken the Children
Bold Me…!

O Thee Love of My Jesus Christ
Hold Me…!

"O" Behold Me Thee Love
"O" Behold Me Thee Kindness

Behold me, to the Thee, of the Lord
Behold Me Thee of Forgiveness

O The Love of My Jesus Christ
Hold Me…!

The Love of Yours the Hearts of Children
Told Me…!

O The Love of My Jesus Christ
Hold Me...!

– Amen

WHO AM I

Have you ever heard a beggar

Cried to the sky
If I am not of the Jesus
Then Who Am I
The thunder to the wind
Whispers the sky
If I am not of the Jesus
Then who am I

The rain that falls on the mountains
Shed tears in the eyes of My

If I am not of the Jesus
Then who am I
The stars shook the moon
The moon raised an above a High
If I am not of the Jesus
Then who am I

The heard of pain the Thou of Thy
Tell the children the those of MY
If I am not of the Children
Then who am I

WHOSE WORDS?

Not my words My little fairy
Not My words
I knock the door Greater Than I
Who is to Listen and Who is to Cry
Not My Words Little Fairy
Not My Words
For I am little Bible in your heart to see

Where comes a way there comes a will to be
Not My Words My Little fairy
Not My Words

For who is there and if not me?
Can u Hear The Thy Speaks Thee
Not My Words Little fairy
Not My Words
For Thou seeks The wisdom?
And The Wisdom Seeks Thy Thee
Not My Words Little Fairy
Not MY Words

Wisdom Sometimes Not All

Once I was a little tree
Green of the leaves
Brown of Thy Thee
Strongest like the mountains
Weak like a Bee
Yes Once I was a little tree

Once I was a little Bird
My Song Never Heard
The tear of forgiveness
The fear of Thy Word
Is there anyone to listen?
Yes Once I was a little Bird

But who is there to the fall?
Green of the Leaves
Songs of the Tall
The knock on the soul
He who speaks of Wisdom
Wisdom sometime not all

THE BEGGAR

The Beggar of One
The Beggar to Many
Silence on the lips
Treasure to any
Distance to the Wise
For the Prayer to rise

So Rough So old
Like a tear of Gold
So Mean so true
The eyes so blue
Cheeks so Frozen
Questions The DO?
The Time is to end!
The Years are few!
The Ladder is of the Wise
A journey to pursue

He who speaks Jesus
The Beggars ask Who?

The NASA Inspire

How would u know
The Sun to Snow
The Snow to Fire
The NASA Inspire
For Every Mission
A Deed Require
The Smile on Our Face

A Humble Desire
The NASA Inspire
How I wonder
Above the Sky
For who is of the Greater
Greater Than I
Courage of Heaven
The Jesus of Thy
The NASA Inspire

THE TIME

The Time is precious
The Time is Untold
Time runs to ponder
The Time is Unsold

Ashes to the Arrogance
Ashes To the Roar
The Time has a life
The Time has a Goal
Time has a meaning
Time Has its Hold
The Time Waits Nothing
The Time is Cold
The Time is Young
The Time is Old
He who dares Challenge
The time is Gold

THE TRUST

How can I bet the wisdom
My Heart Filled with sorrow
For You Have Today

And I have no tomorrow
For You are the Children of Jesus
In Your eyes hidden a faith
For You can only imagine
And I Cannot wait

Trust I, You would win, Thy Lord
For I Am Here only to lose
Long live the children
Forget not You are of whose

THE WISDOM

Who says Love is Bold
Fear is Enemy

Silence is Gold
When bold is after the seek
And Love follows the beak
The Enemy is the of Time
And fear is in the Wine
The Gold is only to Glitter
Silence is when you speak
O Thee Lord of Heaven and the Earth
What Love is when the Prayers are weak?

THE DEED!

How The Grass Is Not So Green?
How The Sky Not So Blue?

How my Lord Loves Me Not!
How My Lord Loves Me True?

Singing to the Walls
Dancing to the Goose

How My Lord Loves Me Not!
How My Lord Loves Me True?

What Is There to Let Smile?
What is There to Let Lose?

How my Lord Loves Me Not!
How my Lord Loves Me True?

Who Is the Christian?
And Who Is the Jew?

How my Lord Loves Me Not!
How my Lord Loves Me True?

Time in Hand Ask You Again
Clock of The Lord is there to begin

What Do You the Must!
What Must Not the DO!

How my Lord Loves Me Not!
How My Lord Loves Me True?

NOTHING A GOLD CAN SAY

The Bold of the dust
The Told of the Rust
The Star that twinkle
The Moon shy's dimple

And the Hope lights the ray

Nothing a Gold Can Say
Nothing a Gold Can Say

When the shine tickles the eye
My Is Yours and You Are My
The Sacred of Bible the Sacred of Thy
The Birds of the Heaven the Song of the Cry

Whoever sings may sing to the Grey

Nothing a Gold Can Say
Nothing a Gold Can Say

For the Gold of Heaven
For the Gold an Above
The world of the silver
The world of the Love

Where there a smile there where the way

Nothing a Gold Can Say
Nothing a Gold Can Say

MISSING THE CHILDREN OF THE CHRIST

How could I count the stars
Missing the Children of the Christ

The Love of Venus the Love of Mars
Missing the Children of the Christ

Some People Stops Some People Last
Missing the Children of the Christ

Who Is Yours and Who Is Ours
Missing the Children OF the Christ

He Who Dares the Door Would Rise
Missing the Children OF the Christ

Who Is Tender and Who has the Light
Missing the Children of the Christ

When Might Surrender the Love Reside

Missing the Children of the Christ

Love Is to Hold Love is to the Right
Missing the Children of the Christ

The Love of Alllah The Love of the Bright
Missing the Children of the Christ

Who Become the Reason Who Has the Sight
Missing the Children of the Christ

May the Wisdom Be of the Right
Missing the Children of the Christ

Blessed Be Those in the Name of Lord
Missing the Children of the Christ

May the Wisdom for Those of God
Missing the Children of Christ

- Amen

MY LORD IS MY LOVE

My Lord is my love
My Lord is my Sorrow

The Words of The Present
The Words of Tomorrow

Who is there to listen
Who is there to borrow

The Promise to be Kept
The Wisdom to be follow

Look Here Stand Thy Jesus
The Song of The Sparrow

My Lord Is My Love
My Lord Is My Sorrow

THE LOVE OF JESUS MY WINE

The pain of the word

The songs you have heard

Shakes me to the time

Yes, The love of Jesus My Wine

You might be sad a little

I wish you see my heart brittle

When words become known to the unknown

Knocking the door before the dawn

I believe the day the star Will Shine

Yes, The love of Jesus My Wine

So let me be who I am

Surrender to the wind who say I am

Finds Me why the shadow of Mine

Yes, The love of Jesus My Wine

Acknowledgments

I would like to express my deepest gratitude to Allah Subhana Tallah and his beloved Jesus Christ, who have guided me throughout my journey as a poet. I am grateful to the team at Atmosphere Press for their dedication and hard work in bringing my poetry book to life. It has been an incredible experience working with such a talented and supportive group of individuals.

Lastly, I appreciate my late father, Prof. Dr. Tahir Hussain, and my mother, Zaitoon Hussain, for their love and prayers that shaped me into the better person I am today.

And lastly, one wonderful lady in my life that I am most grateful to is my friend Ms. Darlene Jones. She is the beautiful reason that gave me support and courage throughout to stand up for myself and publish the songs of my heart in the name of poems. Thank you.

Thank you all and I hope this humble book will bring you joy and inspiration.

About Atmosphere Press

Founded in 2015, Atmosphere Press was built on the principles of Honesty, Transparency, Professionalism, Kindness, and Making Your Book Awesome. As an ethical and author-friendly hybrid press, we stay true to that founding mission today.

If you're a reader, enter our giveaway for a free book here:

SCAN TO ENTER
BOOK GIVEAWAY

If you're a writer, submit your manuscript for consideration here:

SCAN TO SUBMIT
MANUSCRIPT

And always feel free to visit Atmosphere Press and our authors online at atmospherepress.com. See you there soon!

About the Author

Bismillah Hirahmaaan Nira heeem

In the name of God who is most merciful and kind.

Sometimes we are bound to the boundaries of the rain, falling to the mountains, flowing to the rivers, living the message of the sky to every thirst of human cry.

But, who are we, not to surrender to the voice that louds our soul to the key that holds the doors to the wisdom and the roar of the wind.

Must not we find the way where destiny is shaking us to liberate the desire to follow the steps unknown of this world and hereafter and vice versa.

Yes, this humble poet, Farheen Saleem Akhar, was born and brought up in Lahore, Pakistan. Did my Bachelor of Commerce and Master of Computer Sciences from Pakistan too.

But wisdom had more for me to fulfill the thirst that was never filled with what world had to offer me.

I was not the chosen one by the skies to be or not to be who I am today. Perhaps it was a chosen deed of my struggle on to the path of Lord that led me to God's grace and the absolute kindness and love of Allah Subhan. I am grateful to God and His Beloved Christ and the Children that led me deep into the fire of hope and harmony and eventually the desire within faith to where I am today. Alhamdulilllah.

Ever since childhood I was told that all the prophets were the chosen ones by the God and so they did what they were commanded to. Subhan Allah!

It made me realize that every deed needs a commandment to follow and the surrender and reconciliation of the inner self to the wind that follows the sky to the eternal destiny.

But, for the love of God, I chose to be myself and not on to the race of the heavens.

The love of Allah Subhana Tallah showed me the path to the verse of the eternal Holy Bible and The Quran.

The Holy Bible, revealed to God's beloved Jesus Christ, says, "I am the way and the truth and the life. No one comes to the father except through me" (John 14:6).

And The Holy Quran that was revealed to the Prophet Muhammad (Peace be upon him).

Allah Subhan says, "Say, I am a man like you to whom that has been revealed that your God is one God. So whoever would hope for meeting with His Lord, let him do the righteous work and not associate in the worship of his Lord anymore."

These precious and beautiful verses of the God and so many others and all is my struggle toward the path to win the Heart of our Lord and all His beloved Prophets to the righteous way possible in Sha Allah and until I succeed.

The Holy Bible and The Quran are not just books for me to recite to win the way to heaven. It is rather my fairy tale that I lived and danced all my life unknowingly that one day it will become my reality to win my Lord's heart. In Sha Alllah Amen.

The poems written are purely a tribute to the love of Allah Subhana Tallah and His beloved Jesus Christ to the humanity. I am so thankful to God for His blessing on me to express my love and gratitude to my beloved Jesus Christ and His Children. May God bless the Children and all they love, the happiness and the way to His Love, obedience to His word of Heart, a place better than any heaven and more. In Sha Alllah Amen.